SIGRID UNDSET

SIGRID UNDSET

A Study in Christian Realism

by

A. H. WINSNES

Translated
by
P. G. FOOTE

SHEED AND WARD
LONDON AND NEW YORK

FIRST PUBLISHED 1953
BY SHEED AND WARD LTD.
110/111 FLEET STREET
LONDON, E.C.4
AND
SHEED AND WARD, INC.
840 BROADWAY
NEW YORK, 3

PRINTED IN GREAT BRITAIN
BY PURNELL AND SONS, LTD.
PAULTON (SOMERSET) AND LONDON

Foreword

THIS biography of Sigrid Undset was completed a couple of months before her death on June 10th 1949, and is now published without alteration.

While I was working on the book, I had several conversations with her, both about its general plan and on some particular points. "I am delighted that you should want to give me a place in the Christian Renaissance movement" she wrote in a letter dated January 18th 1948. She gave an obliging answer to every question put to her,—most willingly when it was a matter of factual information. She left it to me to find out what she had "meant" in her books. She did me the great service of reading the finished manuscript. In a letter of April 4th 1949, she wrote: "It is difficult to express oneself about a book which has been written about oneself, but I can say that at least I have no objections to make against your interpretation—in the main it is certainly correct."

The interest which Sigrid Undset showed in my work was naturally both an encouragement and an inspiration.

I am further very grateful to all who have helped me in various ways. Amongst others I may mention here Miss Eugenia Kielland and Mrs. Signe Undset Thomas, Sigrid Undset's sister; their work in revision of the manuscript has been of the greatest value.

A. H. WINSNES.

Contents

Contents

Illustrations

Acknowledgment

The passage from *True and Untrue and other Folk Tales*, copyright 1945 by Alfred A. Knopf, Inc., is reprinted by kind permission of the publishers.

Introduction

SIGRID UNDSET'S writing takes its place as one of the truly remarkable phenomena in the literature of the twentieth century. She is, wrote a Swedish critic in 1927, the year before she received the Nobel prize, one of the very few contemporary authors of whom one may well use the adjective "great". That is no exaggeration. In scarcely any of her contemporaries do we find human life treated with comparable breadth of vision and depth of insight. In her thought and imagination, subjects from the present and from distant times are touched by the same convincing assurance and creative power. On her stage she presents characters from the Middle Ages who are as much alive as any of her creations from the present. "I am one who has lived two thousand years in this land" was her remark on a recent ceremonial occasion, with a playful reference to the famous reply of the Government minister, Skogstad, in Gunnar Heiberg's play *I Shall Defend My Country* (*Jeg vil verge mit land*). Sigrid Undset has no relish for the pathetic style, least of all when speaking of herself, but here there was no reserve. Two thousand years—why, it was self-evident! She is in fact not only contemporary with her own time but also with the past, with history. In 1909, two years after her first book *Mrs Marta Oulie* (*Fru Marta Oulie*), a story of married life in an Oslo setting of the most palpable everyday reality, she published *The Story of Viga-Ljot and Vigdis* (*Fortællingen om Viga-Ljot og Vigdis*), a historical novel set in the period at the end of the tenth century. Both books were magnificently alive. An interviewer asked her how it was that she had come to write about characters from such remote times. "One can only write novels about one's own contemporary world" was her answer.

I

Writing about the present and writing about the past do not belong to two distinct periods in her activity as an author, the one a closed chapter followed by the other. There are close links between them all the time. The past is not far away when she writes of the present, nor the present when she writes of the past. Already before her great medieval novels had seen the light of day, in 1919, she was writing to Nini Roll Anker: "I think the reason why I understand our own time so well, or see it so clearly, is because ever since I was a child I have had some kind of living memories from an earlier age to compare with it." In 1905 or thereabouts she had ready the first draft of *Olav Audunsson in Hestviken,* twenty years before the novel was published in its present form.

When Sigrid Undset had published her first book, she received, as a gift from her Danish mother, an edition of *Birds of Passage (Trækfuglene)* by Steen Steensen Blicher. This exhortation was inscribed in it: "May you as an author always look up to Blicher as your model, be as incorruptibly honest as he, fearlessly seeing life as it is and truthfully reporting what you see." And she has written in this way about the present and the past. Could anyone write more truthfully, more realistically?

She does not experiment with new forms of literary expression, with a technique better fitted to grasp concrete realities, in the manner of a Virginia Woolf or a James Joyce. In this respect at least, she is old-fashioned. She carries on the tradition of the great realistic writers of the nineteenth century, Balzac, Dickens, Tolstoy, the style which began in Norway with Camilla Collett and achieved its triumph in Kristian Elster the elder, Alexander Kielland, Jonas Lie and Amalie Skram.

But she is bolder in her description of reality than were most of her great predecessors. The picture she gives of humanity, the passions, hate and love, betrayal and loyalty, the idyllic and the tragic, of the whole of life from the move-

2

ment of the embryo in the womb to the withering of the body and death, from the smell of blood which a human child draws in as it comes into the world up to the highest forms of conscious existence—all this is presented by her without a trace of romantic idealisation or artificiality. Few writers have seen deeper into the unpleasantness of life, into mankind's destitution and wretchedness. We should not close our eyes, she said in a talk to other Catholic writers in America during the last war, to "what a shocking business human life is." But she does not close her eyes to what is most shocking of all: man's own guilty responsibility for his wretchedness. Here too she is without fear; indeed it is in this that her special daring, the boldness she has in greater measure than most of us, is displayed.

Experience of a longing to be nothing more than what we call Nature, without responsibility and without obligation, can come to all of us, she wrote in 1910. "Perhaps we dream that we should live a better and easier life, if our thoughts were to remain at rest, and the hard laws we have imposed on ourselves could be evaded. But then our life would not be human life. And thank the God of us human beings that it is impossible—Nature is not our teacher and neither are the animals."

A notable feature of the cultural life of the twentieth century is the opposition which has made itself felt towards the naturalistic or mechanical deterministic view of humanity, which, from the middle of the last century to the beginning of this, dominated scholarship, philosophy and many branches of literature. Attention is once more paid to man's unique position in the universe. Members of the human species are regarded not only as products of Nature but also as beings with the power to choose and to act in relation to a divine spiritual power behind the visible and material world. The *Hinterweltler*, so despised by Nietzsche, once again come into prominence. The reaction makes itself evident in many ways. In philosophy it takes the form of a liberation from the principal modes of thought which were hostile to metaphysics (metaphysics here implying the recognition of a supernatural reality). The new movement is suggested by names like Bergson, Croce and Whitehead, by the French and German phenomonologists and existentialists, and by neo-Thomists like Maritain and Gilson. Natural science can no longer be used as an arsenal in support of a materialistic world-picture. Characteristic is the tendency amongst biologists, physicists and astronomers to interpret certain natural phenomena as signs of a divine idea in the universe, marks of a reasonable plan or purpose. In history and the social sciences more attention is paid to the organic connection between culture and religion, and to the enormous importance of the religious idea. Arnold Toynbee's great work, *A Study of History*, is conditioned not only by the conception of "the creative spirit of man", but has moreover Augustine's *De Civitate Dei* as its deepest source of inspiration.

But all this is by the way. That which needs special emphasis is the new realism in twentieth-century literature. We are not concerned with the wave of primitivism which poured over Europe in the period after the first World War, perhaps more violently than ever before,—the outlook representative of the phalanx of "life-worshippers", the true anti-intellectuals, who saw creative and rejuvenating power only in the "blood", in the impulses and instincts. Nor are we concerned with that group of writers who have not unreasonably been given the name of Post-Naturalists, those who find in Marx and Freud assurance of the soul's imprisonment within the confines of naturalism. Here we speak rather of a series of writers who, independently or because of the influence of Bergson or Freud or both, have had their attention directed to deeper layers of the mind than could be grasped by the "hard-boiled" school of psychologists. It is their intention to capture not only

4

the physical but also the spiritual. Typical amongst them are authors like Virginia Woolf, James Joyce, Aldous Huxley, Rainer Maria Rilke, Franz Kafka, Marcel Proust, Sigurd Christiansen, Tarjei Vesaas, Harry Martinson, and Aksel Sandemose.

At first glance, the robust realism of Sigrid Undset may seem to stand far removed from the writing of this group. It would be difficult to conceive a greater disparity, as far as the means of artistic presentation are concerned, than that between James Joyce and Franz Kafka on the one side and Sigrid Undset on the other, or, to choose a Norwegian author, between Sigurd Christiansen and Sigrid Undset. With Christiansen one finds an intense concentration on the inner mental processes of a single character, and little attention is paid to the outer world. Sigrid Undset probes no less deeply into the inner life, but her work shows too that breadth of background description which is typical of the realistic novel, and the sharpest possible insight into the conditions imposed on the characters by their social position and mileu. There are however points of contact, for example in the essential part which memory, the great mysterious factor in our mental life, plays in the writing of these authors. And further, not all of these "Neo-Realists" lose themselves in the subconscious world or in the sub-human; they are brought face to face with what is specifically human: the spiritual in man. The religious factor, the craving for eternity, asserts itself. To take a single example amongst many we may name Franz Kafka, one of the great religious writers of our time.

In her outlook, however, Sigrid Undset's closest connection with present-day literature and the whole contemporary world of ideas is not to be found in the movement here briefly described. It lies rather on a broader plane, is less purely literary and closer to the common stuff of humanity; it is to be sought in that Christian-inspired movement which has expressed itself in many ways in twentieth-century thought, and which in literature has made itself so firmly felt that it has rightly been called a Christian Renaissance.

A Christian Renaissance in the twentieth century? It sounds paradoxical. The opposition which Christianity has faced perpetually since its foundation,—more than any other of the great world-religions,—has never appeared more aggressive than in this period, the century of Communism, Fascism and Nazism. The fight waged against the Church by Voltaire, in the eighteenth century, for example, was not prompted by any ideological hostility to the Christian ethical values. Jesus of Nazareth is the Master, because in His eyes all men are equal, are the words in the *Dictionnaire Philosophique*[1]. The paganism of the twentieth century, on the other hand, sees in the Christian religion the decisive, indeed the essential, obstacle to the realisation of its programme for human society. It attacks the entire Christian faith: and not without cause, for it seeks also to destroy the Christian ethic.

This intensified struggle against Christianity is certainly one of the reasons for the Christian re-awakening of our time. The repudiation of Christianity, which had been formerly a part of the enthusiastic and optimistic faith in "progress" and which was largely a product of intellectual debating-circles, entered a new phase when great nations began to put this idea of the abolition of the Christian faith into practice. With reference to his visit to Soviet Russia, André Gide writes, "Ignorance and denial of the Gospel and of all that has followed from it cannot but lead to the impoverishment of humanity and culture." But the Christian movement in modern literature is not the outcome of panic. It is important to recollect that its roots go deeper than the first World War and the explosions which opened the floodgates to the modern paganism. To writers and thinkers in many countries it had long been clear what the repudiation of Christianity and the general secularisation

---

[1] Alfred NOYES, *Voltaire*, London 1936, p. 638.

of humanity would entail. In an article called *War and Literature* Sigrid Undset writes, with reference to this, "It happens that a writer seems to see in advance the gloom through which we must pass—'the dark places'—and seeks to find a way out."

The Christian writing and thought of the twentieth century possess a markedly realistic, sometimes almost anti-romantic, character. They have nothing in common with that "retreat from the world" which was at times the chief feature of the so-called literary conversions of the late nineteenth century. Admittedly, no one would think of classifying as mere superficial products of their age the Jacob's wrestle of August Strindberg, Léon Bloy's burning witness, the profound Catholic faith of Johannes Jørgensen, or Arne Garborg's restless search for some God to believe in. But these do not possess that intimate contact with reality which characterises the twentieth-century group of Christian writers and thinkers. There is an upsurge of healthiness in this group, a deep love for the normal and eternally human and for ordinary common sense. The lyric poetry of Paul Claudel is a hymn to the sensible concrete world, God's creation, and is sustained by the Psalmist's theme: the heavens show forth the glory of God. The religious poetry of Olav Aukrust, revealing Christian influence as it does, yet shows the divine acknowledgment side by side with the richest sensuousness. G. K. Chesterton's apology for the Christian religion sparkles with wit, humour and down-to-earth humanity. T. S. Eliot binds poetry to the realities of contemporary social life in a way which not only means a revolution in verse-technique, but also—and this is the important point—unveils the everlasting banality of a God-forsaken world: The Waste Land. But there is no *Weltschmerz*. The created holds within itself a message from the Creator: "We praise Thee, O God, for Thy glory displayed in all the creatures of the earth." In their vital concern with contemporary problems, the new Christian thinkers, with Bergson as one of their forerunners and with Maritain, Gilson, Scheler, Berdiaev and others numbered amongst them, are raising the central question of all philosophy. *Philosophia perennis*, the doctrine that mankind belongs essentially to a supernatural world of the spirit, scarcely occupies the weakest bastion in twentieth-century thought. Modern society is analysed and criticised, but the criticism is animated by a living consciousness of the tradition behind it. Past and future are bound together, thanks to "the Christian road we have discovered" (Charles Péguy). And it is no less important that man does not take for granted the conviction that, when there is something wrong, the fault lies outside himself. Someone, writes Sigrid Undset, had to be led to the thought "that there is nothing wrong with the world other than the will of man" (in a private letter, dated January 18th 1948). The novels of François Mauriac, Georges Bernanos, Graham Greene, Evelyn Waugh and Sigrid Undset herself, to mention a few amongst many, give some of the most penetrating psychological studies of our time, often agonising in their merciless unveiling. They show us perhaps the least popular picture of mankind, man as "the architect of his own misfortune", to quote Sigrid Undset again. Paul Valéry writes that the Christian religion demands self-examination; it "sets the human mind to the most subtle of problems, the most important and the most fruitful." It is scarcely an exaggeration to say that psychological realism begins in earnest with the *Confessions* of Saint Augustine.

Sigrid Undset is the Christian realist *par excellence*. More than any other writer she gathers together the threads of the European realist tradition. Her writing has grown organically out of the powerful presentation of everyday reality which we meet in the nineteenth-century novel and which is the essence of literary realism. But the preconditions go further back in time, to Shakespeare and his contemporaries and to Chaucer. "One thinks of Dickens when one reads Chaucer," she writes, ". . . they are closely related, both were realists who described the actuality they found before them—and it was a better actuality than we can find." And her roots go back to the Icelandic family-sagas. She once described the reading of *Njáls Saga* as a turning-point in her life. It was precisely the intense realism of the saga which gripped her. But gradually the Christian point of view becomes decisive for her presentation of life, the attitude which gives to the ordinary average man a completely new significance, placing on him an emphasis quite unknown in non-Christian thinking. The realism of Christianity is indomitable, she writes. Even as a school-girl she had been impressed by the realism of the stories in the Bible. It was by virtue of her Christian outlook that she learnt to see all human relationships not in isolation and abstraction but collectively, to see her characters not only in relation to the commonplace, to the age or society in which they lived, but also as creatures in relation to the Creator, and then to treat this motive, as she herself says, "as a fact just as realistic as any erotic impulse or longing for earthly happiness,"

CHAPTER I

Childhood and Youth

SIGRID UNDSET was born in Kalundborg in Vest-Sjælland on May 20th 1882. In her veins flowed Norwegian, Danish and Scottish blood, and through the extensive branches of her family she was related to such noble characters as Petter Dass, Tordenskjold, Johan Herman Wëssel and Johan Falkberget.

Her father, the famous archæologist Ingvald Undset, came of a backwoods family in Sollia in Østerdal. They had the reputation of being "tough and headstrong folk". One member of the family, Sigrid Undset's grandfather, married a daughter from the farm Undset in Øvre Rendal; he died young and she returned to Undset. Halvor Undset, their son, did not take up farming but went to the training school for non-commissioned officers in Trondheim; he became a colour-sergeant and warden of the penal labour settlement at Vollan.

Halvor Undset was a very religious man, perhaps somewhat sectarian, but in essentials completely at one with the Church. As a small girl, Sigrid Undset was impressed by the deep sincerity of her grandfather's faith in God's will and his surrender to it. In her volume of childhood reminiscences, *Eleven Years*, she says that it almost terrified her. "It was somehow frightening that a man could *love* God as grandfather did." Both he and his wife would doubtless have preferred that their gifted son, Ingvald, who matriculated with distinction from the Cathedral School in Trondheim in 1871, should have chosen to study theology at the University rather than classical and Scandinavian philology. But when the interests and talents of their son pointed in another direction, they resigned themselves to it. They were delighted to hear of his progress and proud of the name he won for himself, not least abroad, as an archæologist. Sigrid Undset remembered once seeing her grandfather sit and look through the folio which contained all the letters from the foreign academies which had elected his distinguished son a member. "Grandfather nodded his head a little over each one. Good Trøndelag folk as they were, the old people certainly had that ineradicable feeling about 'foreign parts'. One could foster as deep a suspicion as one wished about everything in 'the great world' outside,— all the same, praise and fame from abroad were nearly the greatest a Norwegian could achieve" (*Eleven Years*).

Even as a boy Ingvald Undset reacted against much he saw in the clerical and lay "shepherds" who were for ever visiting his home in Vollan. Later, when he thought back on the various sides of their character, he could say, "The Catholics were content with a single Pope, and he was only infallible when he spoke *ex cathedra*, but the Christian circles of friends here in the north gladly accepted popes by the dozen, and they were infallible no matter whether they spoke in the chapel or over a well-spread dinner-table, standing in the pulpit or in their galoshes" (*Eleven Years*).

Ingvald Undset won his international reputation with the epoch-making work, *The Beginnings of the Iron Age in Northern Europe* (1881). He had however been an active archæologist since boyhood. He was one of those happy souls, writes the archæologist and historian Henrik H. Mathiesen, "who, when the hour comes, are never for a moment in doubt as to what work they will dedicate themselves to." Ingvald Undset and Henrik Mathiesen were constant friends from their school-days. They were thrown together from the start, for both of them had their heads full of Snorri, P. A. Munch and Trondheim Cathedral. The two boys played at "research" in the cathedral until they

knew every nook and cranny, the partly covered passages
in the walls and the inscriptions on the floors. Later in life
they often worked in cooperation and in the summer of
1888 they went on a research trip together. Sigrid Undset
heard them talk afterwards of the "great journey", as they
called it. They began amongst the cathedral ruins at Hamar,
went on up to the church at Ringsaker, and so on over to
Toten and Valdres, passing from one runic stone to the
next. In 1890, a couple of years before his death, Ingvald
Undset wrote a small popular study, *The First Beginnings
of the Oslo Valley*. The ordinary person, he says there, rarely
thinks of how things looked here thousands of years ago,
before the first human being set foot in this area: but it is
different with the archæologist, "who in his thoughts and
investigations has accustomed himself to seeking far back
to the first beginnings".

Ingvald Undset was not anti-religious. He may perhaps
be characterised most accurately as an agnostic with an
impulse towards religious faith and with a deep respect for
Christianity. It may be that it was especially from his way
of talking about religion that Sigrid Undset as a child got
the impression that there was something true in all religious
conceptions,—as if, down through the ages, people had been
able to grasp more and more of something they really knew
but found difficult to express. His book of travels, *From
Akershus to the Acropolis*, gives us an interesting glimpse into
the world of his thoughts. The section, "Perspectives of
World History", has an individual, personal flavour, and
reads now like a foreshadowing of the imaginative writing
which his then unborn daughter was to create. There we
find this: "Slowly we return homeward, our thoughts busy
with what was perhaps the most interesting and significant
period in all history, the time when the ancient world sank
into the dust and Christianity rose up to become a world-
power. We go under the arch of Constantine and pass by
the Coliseum, the mightiest remnant of antiquity in this

Rome so full of ruins; and herein many a martyr bled for
the new faith, which had its source in the carpenter's son
from Nazareth and which the ancient world found itself
compelled to fight with fire and sword. But the now doctrine
was victorious; on the ruins of the world-empire of ancient
Rome there was built through its agency a new world-
domination, different in character from the first, but more
lasting and stronger, still stronger today than most believe.
Even for the stoutest unbeliever, Christianity in its external
activity and power must still remain the most significant
factor in the development of the world. You may have
visited Rome, entirely occupied with an interest in the
ancient world and its remains, but if you have any real
sense of the development of the human race as a whole,
you will soon come to look with no less interest on the
remains of the second Rome which lie deposited on those
of the first, remains of the world-capital of the ancient
Church and papal dominion."

Ingvald Undset's gifted daughter grew more and more
fascinated by her father's work, and already before she
could talk properly, babbled of "thick-necked" and "shaft-
hole" axes, and played with the little terracotta horse from
Troy which Schliemann had given to her father. It was
his dream that she should become a scholar when she
grew up, and continue his own work. That dream was not
fulfilled in precisely the way he had imagined, but in
different form and in richer measure than he could ever
have suspected. She was in her twelfth year when he died
in 1893.

Ingvald Undset met his wife-to-be, Anna Charlotte Gyth,
when he was a student in Copenhagen in the 1870's. Her
father, a chancery councillor in Kalundborg, came of one
of the Scottish families who had settled in North Norway
in the seventeenth century. The Danish branch of the
family had come from Norway to Copenhagen with Sigrid
Undset's great-great-grandfather, Anders Broch Gyth, who

had tried his luck in the capital of the "twin kingdoms". He was present at the execution of Struensee and in letters home to Hellesviken in Helgeland described the impression made on him by this catastrophe. Luck was not with him; he could never afford to make the journey back to Norway, and his descendants were Danish. His grandson, the father of Sigrid Undset's mother, became a prominent man in Kalundborg; he had a considerable legal practice and estate agency, was prosperous, and greatly respected for his upright character and willingness to lend a helping hand. The Imperial-style house of the chancery councillor still stands, with its clean peaceful lines and the tall linden trees casting their shadows over the white façade and high stone steps. His wife, a daughter of Dean Vilhelm Adolf Worsøe, died when Charlotte Gyth, Sigrid Undset's mother, was a little girl. Signe Dorthea Worsøe, an elder sister of his dead wife, came to keep house for the widower and the six motherless children. She made a "cruel distinction" between the children, preferring the prettiest and most lively and cheerful at the expense of the others. Charlotte was her favourite and she spoiled her beyond all reason.

Charlotte Gyth was an intelligent, self-willed and capricious little creature, who admired her husband, took a lively interest in his work and accompanied him on his travels abroad. "She had the kind of intelligence which makes it easy for a person to learn anything he or she wants to learn, and it pleased her to work with a young enamoured husband and to have the opportunity of travelling and seeing so much" (*Eleven Years*). She never came to feel at home in Norway. People thought the small-town lady, who was made so much of, somewhat superior. For her part, she was inclined to look down on conditions in the provincial capital. She was temperamental, with decided preferences and antipathies. If she did not care for someone, she took no trouble to hide the fact. Mrs Mathilde Hassel, who was then Mathilde Klaveness, got to know

ANNA CHARLOTTE UNDSET (*née* GYTH), 1893

INGVALD UNDSET, *circa* 1885

Charlotte Gyth when she came, newly engaged, to Oslo and lived in I. M. Nielsen's boarding-house. Mrs Hassel was not only charmed by her person and impressed by her accomplishments (amongst them was Charlotte's excellent command of French), but also realised what a woman of distinction and value she was. "Anna Charlotte had something unusual about her." Nils Collett Vogt, who met Mrs Undset when she was considerably older, was captivated by her brilliant and witty conversation. She preserved an air of *la grande dame*, even in the days of poverty and adversity. She had something of an eighteenth-century quality and it was indeed that period which represented her ideal. There she belonged in her opinions, ideas and literary interests. "To regard the world with the sanity of a rationalist and everything human with a benign scepticism,—that was the ideal which for Anine [the name given her in *Eleven Years*] was easier to possess than practise." As far as religious and political matters were concerned, she was neither radical nor conservative. She grew furious with people who wanted to preserve everything which mere custom and convention had made sacrosanct. But she reacted just as fiercely at the sentimentality which she found in the "cock-crowing of a new dawn" of the radicals. Later in life she became a Catholic. She was punctilious in performing readily and completely all her religious duties. She read Thomas Aquinas with enthusiasm. She thought that in him she discovered for the first time what true humanism is. She kept her sense of humour to the end. It is a wonderful thing to pray to Our Lord, she said; it's like telephoning—often there is no reply.

Charlotte Undset found it difficult to take to strangers, but she loved her children and home all the more intensely; her mother-love was strong and passionate. When she was left on her own after her husband's death, with three small daughters and a meagre widow's pension for her only assistance, her will grew like steel. The Undsets' home continued to be a little life-giving workshop of humanity and culture. The widow Mrs Wegener in *Spring* (*Vaaren*) bears some resemblance to Sigrid Undset's mother. Of Mrs Wegener the book says that she fostered the minds and thoughts of her children, poured out from her own abundance, from the poetry that filled her, a transcendant richness and splendour, which her children sucked greedily in.

When in 1880 Ingvald Undset had to turn back because of illness from his Mediterranean travels, the newly-married couple settled down in Kalundborg, living in one wing of the house of Charlotte's father. Here Sigrid Undset spent the first two years of her life. She had some recollection of that time—it was something "like a perpetual basking on warm earth in the sun" (*Eleven Years*). In 1884 the family returned to Norway. At first they lived in a house set in a large enclosure in the neighbourhood of Vestre Aker church. Then they moved to Number Ten in the idyllic Lyder Sagens Street, also in a district "on the border between town and country, on the one side Vestre Aker which was still farming-land, on the other Oslo which, great city though it was, still extended no further", as Sigrid Undset writes in *The Falling Source* (*Strømmen tyner*). She continues: "We could feel the year's cycle as an ebb and flow of the forces of growth. To us Nature did not mean *places* to which we made excursions, but a huge body which we could see arching itself in the light of dawn; in the noon heat it breathed and stared at us, with a tangible exterior and an interior of unplumbed mystic depth; it could be touched and felt like an animal, but remained enigmatic. And in the evening, the world turned over on its side, dozed off into the darkness of the night, and heaved out strange sounds as it dreamed."

The years in Lyder Sagens Street were happy ones, though the early stage of her father's sickness cast a slight shadow over existence there. But with the healthy instinct of a child for making the best of things, she kept all the disquieting signs at a distance. It was indeed a "golden childhood". Then came sudden reversal. Her father's advancing illness made it necessary for him to find a home nearer the University Museum. The family moved into the crowded town, to Number Five, Keysers Street. The new apartment was gloomy, and the tragic course of her father's disease became more and more apparent. Stifling impressions and feelings of disgust were forced on the child's mind. Now and then she could fairly revel in her melancholy. Nevertheless, in the dark cellars and court-yards there were strange and exciting places to play in, and there were glimpses to be had of a world outside the walls of home, a world which had seemed quite irrelevant when they were living in Lyder Sagens Street. She was enchanted by the whole area round the old cathedral school, Trinity Church, Saint Olav's Church and Hammersborg. "That was the true Oslo," she writes in her fascinating description of this part of the town in *Eleven Years*: "—in some ways a melancholy part, but homely and nowhere uninteresting." But it did seem dull to her when they moved to Observatory Street on the western side of the town, where in her opinion people were not free from snobbishness. The children talked of things which she had been taught to regard as foolish subjects for discussion— whether, for example, it was more elegant to go to Miss Conradi's school or to Miss Bonnevie's. She was happy when, after her father's death, the family moved to Steens Street, with the slopes and rocks of Blaasen near at hand; from it a few minutes' scamper would bring her to her beloved old Lyder Sagens Street.

Even though she lived in several parts of the town, each one with its own characteristic features, she never had a feeling of not belonging. Her home was always the place to which she could return for refuge with absolute confidence; it seemed to have a fluidity which embraced her wherever she went. And it was, she says, the same with the other children she knew.

There was little sentimentality in the way she was brought up. She paid no real heed if her mother gave her an occasional smack in order to get her out of some bad habit or to improve her manners. Her mother's temper was accepted just like the weather: it was a nuisance when it was bad, otherwise there was nothing more to be said about it. But she once got a beating from her father—she had told lies about her younger sister—and then she had to think seriously of what she had done.

There was in her upbringing nothing beyond what was conventionally religious. On Christmas Eve the Christmas Gospel was read aloud, and her mother taught her to say the evening prayer:

> *Now our eyes are closing,*
> *Heavenly Father, on high disposing,*
> *Protect me through this night;*
> *From danger, sin and sorrow*
> *Thine angel guard us till tomorrow,*
> *Who watched us in the light.*
> *Amen for Jesus' sake.*

"Our eyes" in the first line she could never understand as her own, but those of God who sat up in the clouds and saw everything. The evening prayer came to play a part in all her ideas of what religion meant. She had grown used to saying it with her mother, but without understanding what she said. One evening their mother was out and the girls lay alone and frightened in the dark nursery. The nursemaid came in. "Now say your prayers nicely and then you needn't be afraid of anything" she said and went out again. It seemed to the child almost unsafe to say the prayer by herself, but she set her mind to it. In *Eleven Years* Sigrid Undset remarks on this in a way which hints at something fundamental in her religious sensibility. She said the

SIGRID UNDSET AT THE AGE OF 1

evening prayer, she writes, with a feeling that she was embarking on a hazardous adventure, like going somewhere she had never been before. Somehow or other she felt as if she had become much bigger after she had dared to say the prayer by herself. "Alone with the Alone" are the words in which an English mystic describes his religious experience.

She interpreted the weather signals hoisted on Sankthanshaugen as signals or messages from God, indicating His pleasure or displeasure with mankind. "When she saw that only the triangle had been hoisted, then the sunshine and the clear blue sky became, as it were, the benevolence of God Himself spread out over the earth and trees and all men: now He was pleased with everything at once. But the square was a symbol which seemed to show that He had drawn the clouds between Himself and the world; He was in a bad humour and had turned away, and the child was despondent when she saw it. The square hoisted above the triangle appeared worst of all, for it meant that something had happened at that moment to anger God, and the signal showed that it might be some time before He was amenable again. But it was wonderful when the triangle was seen above the square—it was as if the whole world had been told 'All is forgiven'; God was friends with us again and now there would only be sunshine and good temper,—until the next time something cropped up" (*Eleven Years*). A psychologist who maintains that the religious attitude is secondary or derivative will perhaps see in this a typical instance of a childish projection of the fear of *pater familias*.

The strong simple natural images in Ingemann's morning and evening hymns, which their mother sang for the children, filled her childish mind with reverent wonder, but most of the hymns she had later to sing in service at school occasioned in her a positive aversion. They seemed sentimental and self-centred, and did not make her think "of God as One behind the cycle of day and night and the seasons. So long as He stayed *there*, she could think of Him respectfully and reverently, and with gratitude too for the light and the wind and everything that tasted or smelt good. But she had absolutely no desire for Him to be too much concerned with her behaviour and thoughts" (*Eleven Years*).

She reacted instinctively and firmly against any attempt to spoonfeed her with a cosy and comfortable religion. She felt that God was just the opposite of everything of that kind. A sense of the holy lay at the centre of the child's germinating and half-conscious religious life.

It was a pure accident that she went to church while still a child. One Sunday—she must have been nine or ten—the maid had told her she ought to go to church: "You who have only to cross the road and you're there! But there's no one in this house who ever dreams of going to God's house on a Sunday. I'm amazed that you're not ashamed of yourself, I am." It had its effect on the little girl. She went into Trinity Church. The organ-music and the hymn-singing made an impression on her, but it was completely destroyed when the priest went up into the pulpit. "She could make nothing of what he said, even though in fact he repeated words and whole sentences over and over again. And then he spoke in such a strange way, now his voice would rise as high as could be and then sink right down again; and sometimes he put such a peculiar emphasis on the words. She sat there feeling embarrassed: it was as if he was making an exhibition of himself" (*Eleven Years*).

Once at home again, she was reluctant to say she had been to church. But when they were at dinner, she thought she must announce, "I've been to Trinity Church." "You went to church?" said her mother; "why, that was an odd thing to do—what made you think of it?" "Well, I had never been before." "Oh yes" said her mother reflectively. "But you didn't have a hymnbook, did you?—If you think

of going again, you must take a hymnbook with you"
(*Eleven Years*). She tried going to church once more, but
only once.

The Undset family had no great circle of acquaintances
in Oslo, but Ingvald Undset's friends and colleagues were
frequent visitors, amongst them Sophus Bugge, Ernst Sars,
Ludvig Daae and S. Laache, the specialist in internal
disorders, Ingvald Undset's doctor and certainly his closest
friend. Naturally they discussed politics, the Right and
Left, the Supreme Court, Bjørnson and Sverdrup and the
tax on books. Sigrid Undset did not find these "feasts of
talk" so interesting, but she listened spell-bound when
the conversation got round to archæological and historical
subjects, ancient trade-routes, runic inscriptions, the age of
the Eddic poems, the riddles of the Golden Horn of Gallehus
and the Røk stone. A book by Japetus Steenstrup gave rise
to a whole evening's discussion on the runic alphabet in
the Black Sea region.

When her father grew weaker and was confined to his
wheel-chair, Sigrid read aloud to him. At first she was a
little hesitant, but she was gripped by what she read, even
if it was only half understood. When she fancied she had
really grasped something, she pressed blithely on—even
when it was a verse in Old Norse. Sometimes she was vain
enough to think how clever she was; at other times she
forgot everything except that the poetry was so splendid
that it made her shiver with delight:

Drag þú mér af hendi	*Draw from my arm*
hring enn rauða,	*the ring so red,*
fær þú enni ungu	*carry it back*
Ingibjǫrgu.	*to Ingibjörg.*
Sá mun henni	*It will be to her*
hugfastr tregi,	*a deep-set grief,*
er ek eigi kem	*when I return not*
til Uppsala.	*to Uppsala.*

The last piece she read for him, on the day before he died, was *Hávarðar Saga Ísfirðings*. In some parts she expected that he would ask her to read it in the Old Icelandic, but when he said nothing she realised that he must be very tired. Next day when her mother came out of the sick-room, she saw at once on her face what had happened. Their mother took the children into the little room for them to see: their father lay dead in his bed.

Sigrid Undset was set in the midst of living traditions. We loved these traditions so dearly, she says in *The Failing Source (Strømmen tyner)*, because deep down we knew from what a noble source they sprang, a source moreover which might perhaps soon dry up. "If we did not believe directly in fairies, goblins and trolls—we believed in ghosts as a matter of course, but then we had not been so injured by our powers of observation as to become materialists—we at least believed in the living mother of all such." The tales of Asbjørnson and Moe and Elling Holst's picture-book were in this way not to be classed with other children's books, with Bernt Lie and Dikken Zwilgmeyer.

Both her father and mother used to tell stories, for the most part tales which they made up as they went along. But on the ground-floor of the villa in Lyder Sagens Street, beneath the home of the Undsets, there lived an old lady, Anna Winter-Hjelm, born in Germany and the wife of Winter-Hjelm the organist. In *Eleven Years* she is called Mrs Wilster. There were ten children in the Winter-Hjelms' home, and each one of them had friends, boys and girls, who were for ever running in and out. Mrs Winter-Hjelm sat there with her darning-basket or sewing-machine, or else preparing vegetables; she was never without children round her. In the summer she took them for country walks. The fairy-tale tradition was deeply alive in her, and she told tales which could scare the little ones out of their wits or make them shriek with laughter. And the nursemaid, Caroline Thorvaldsen, who came of families in Smaalenene and Drøbak, told fairy-tales from the eastern part of the country, and drew on an overwhelming rich ness of fantasy. Sigrid Undset writes of her, "At story-telling she was a past-master above all others." But didn't "Moster"[1] in Kalundborg outdo her?—for she must have been an unsurpassed teller of tales. There was nothing placed in the way of the satisfaction of this hunger for stories. It was not accepted as a peda-gogic principle that the child's mental life should be rendered barren. Mrs Winter-Hjelm, Caroline Thorvaldsen and "Moster" were able to sow their seeds unhindered in the childish mind of Norway's greatest woman story-teller.

She loved to be the narrator herself. Those who knew her best could not help becoming aware of her visionary fantasy and inventive power. At night, when the three sisters had gone to bed, Sigrid, the eldest, began to tell stories which stretched themselves out from one evening to the next; the characters were usually the same, but they were continually having new fantastic experiences. At an early age she showed an amazing ability to give characters to her purely imaginary creations, and she amused herself also by drawing them and pasting them onto match-boxes to create in this way a complete puppet-theatre (*Aften-posten*, May 14th 1928).

Their mother exercised control over the children's read-ing. She could not stand children's books full of senti-mental moralising. Sigrid Undset was certainly not allowed to sit about and linger over "such rubbish"—"Out and play!" But her mother had no objection to the juicy humour of "Daddy" Holberg and Johan Herman Wessel. The children knew *Peder Paars* almost by heart. As time went on, Sigrid Undset became familiar with Holberg's world and characters, so that they too became homely and dear

[1] Signe Dorothea Worsøe.

to her, as Hans Andersen, Asbjørnson and the ballads (the Danish especially at first) already were.

The summer holidays yielded intense experiences which left bright clear pictures in her memory. The summer months spent at Kalundborg, in Østerdal or Trøndelag, Drøbak or Hvitsten, where the family often rented a house for the holidays, seemed times detached from all other time. She could recall sensations and moods which were inextricably bound up one with another. Her grandfather's old gardens in Kalundborg were enchanting. "One came into an air which was a surfeit of scents—bitter-sweet from the box-hedges, cool and pure from the phlox, and the rank sweaty smell from elder and ivy. . . . Then there were spiders of every shape and size, fat blue-bottles that flashed as they skimmed out of the shade into the sunshine, and the terrifying earwigs. . . . But the gloom under the old trees and the mystical insects only made the gardens more fascinating in my eyes" (*Christmas in Kalundborg and District* 1946; *Jul i Kalundborg og omegn* 1946). She remembered the fairy-tale evenings in Kalundborg best from the summer of 1887, when she was just five years old; they stayed there longer than usual because there had been an outbreak of diphtheria in Lyder Sagens Street. She and her sisters had a bedroom overlooking the square. Even on a summer evening, the magnificent great linden trees outside made the room dark early. "Moster came in, quickly and quietly, small and nimble as a mouse,—the tiny trains with which she always had her dresses made rendered the likeness even more striking. She settled herself in the seat by the window, lifted her knitting high under her nose in the gloom, and peered over her spectacles at the two of us in bed: 'Now, my little snails, what shall we have for a story tonight?'" One of her stories, Søll-Klara, has been given by Sigrid Undset in *The Failing Source* as she herself used to tell it to Norwegian children.

And then the summers north of the Dovre mountains!

Her father always thought of himself as a native of Trøndelag, and she too was always overcome by a deep and joyful
sense of recognition when the journey eventually brought
her down the long valleys to Trondheimofjord. Best of all
she remembered the summer of 1891, the last summer she
spent there with her father. She sat at the carriage-window
opposite him as the train came down through the Gaul
valley. She knew all the names from history, Lunde, Rimul,
Gimsar, Medalhus, and her father told her where the farms
lay. She absorbed the whole landscape, the dark-green
fields, the white washing spread outside a farm with big
outhouses, the farmhouse itself long and brightly painted.
"New-laundered clothes spread out on a green field seemed
to be her earliest and tenderest impression of Trøndelag"
are her words. But never before had she realised how lovely
the summer can be in Norway.

It was in her grandfather's library at Vollan that she came
upon a copy of *Njáls Saga* in Sommerfelt's translation. It
went completely to her head. She would wake up in the
morning, dress and sit at breakfast, sick with impatience
to lay her hands on the book again and get outside to a place
where she could continue her reading. Both in *Eleven Years*
and later in a little essay in English, *A Book That Was a
Turning-Point in My Life*, she has described in detail this
first encounter with the Icelandic family-saga. She would
lie out in the green bleaching-field and read. Now and
then she was forced to put the book away from her to give
her time to absorb what she had read, or to give her a
chance to cool her burning face down in the grass. Everything lived so vividly before her eyes that it almost hurt:
Skarpheðin especially, reckless and unstable, with his pale
sallow-brown face, his dark eyes and beard. She could not
understand what was the matter with him. Whenever
the others had brought about a reconciliation and everything seemed to be going well, Skarpheðin, white-faced and
behaving like a madman, came and destroyed it all. But

she had, she says, a sort of premonition of how women could come to link their destinies with those of gifted misfits or neurotics.

Another such summer, one that was to remain indelibly imprinted on her memory, she experienced in Drøbak—in whose neighbourhood we are to imagine the situation of Olav Audunsson's farm, Hestviken. It was the year after her father's death, so that she was twelve or thirteen. The painter, Theodor Kittelsen, lived nearby, and at that time she was fully determined to be an artist when she grew up; she drew incessantly, both at home and at school. She was particularly enthusiastic about Chr. Krohg and Weren-skiold, but this summer in Drøbak they both had to give place to Kittelsen. She was in and out of his house all the time, where she found every wall covered with paintings and sketches. She discovered there in living form the whole world of all the whimsical and wonderful creatures she had heard tell of in legend and fairy-tale. Kittelsen looked at her drawings and was convinced that she had talent; he advised her to study painting when she had finished at school. One summer in Hvitsten there was the flame of a little childish romance. In *Eleven Years* his name is Olaf. "As I remember it," she writes, "there seemed to be sunshine every single day that summer."

Sigrid Undset was given her first lessons at home by her mother, but when she had reached third-form standard she was sent to Ragna Nielsen's school. Her father was a Liberal and had no misgivings about letting her go to the radical Liberal school. Sigrid Undset was struck by Ragna Nielsen's beauty—and she was always so handsomely dressed, in dark-coloured or light grey gowns, with a broad white bib which made the dress look like a kind of uniform. She inspired respect in the highest degree. Sigrid found it exciting to attend this radical school, although, it was true, Olaf, her friend from Hvitsten, had talked scorn-

fully of boys and girls going to the same school. He had
also left her with the suspicion that the Conservatives were
not as black as they were painted: he said that all sailors
were conservative. And on the seventeenth of May[1] it was
certainly a fine thing to go in the children's procession, with
the single flag everywhere, and sing Bjørnson's national
songs.

All the same she felt some dissatisfaction with the school.
Think for yourselves, said the teachers, but if she did and
came to a conclusion other than that properly prescribed as
radical, she was always wrong. At home she had learnt that
the world of learning was always in motion, but at school
the teachers were so "remarkably certain of the letter of
the law" when it came to the final results of scholarship.
As for God, she got the impression that they believed He
was a great almighty Liberal, who stood by co-education
and the single flag. She is without doubt essentially correct
when she says that, already as a thirteen-year-old, she had
seen through the radicalism of the 'eighties. Something
central in her comprehension of life had dawned on her:
she saw that the more people freed themselves from religious
dogmas, the easier it was for them to bind themselves to
political doctrines.

Sigrid Undset had few friends as a girl. She attached
herself to only one of her schoolfellows, Emma Münster,
and then not until her last year at school. Emma Münster,
who afterwards became a doctor, would seem to be the only
woman friend Sigrid Undset ever had who was completely
in tune with her. The two schoolgirls had common ground
in their passion for botany, and they roamed the country-
side round Oslo collecting flowers. These trips laid the
foundations of Sigrid Undset's quite remarkable botanical
knowledge, and this hobby probably gave her more pleasure
than any other. About three-quarters of every letter she

[1] Norway's Independence Day, the anniversary of the ratification of an
independent constitution by the National Assembly at Eidsvole in 1814.

wrote to her sister Signe from her exile in America dealt
with the plant-life she found there.

Religious instruction was one of the things she found least
dull at school. Naturally there was a good deal in the Old
Testament that aroused no response. "One must be completely grown up to perceive anything of the power which
lies in the story of Job, or to be gripped by the light and
dark, the idyllic and tragic, in the story of David." But
she felt that the biblical stories dealt with men who were
truly alive. "It was not disguised that, although King
David was both hero and poet, he was capable of mean
actions, or that the reckless Samson was considerably braver
than wise, or that the prophets could sulk and whine in
their self-pity" (*On Abraham's Sacrifice; Omkring Abrahams
offer*).

Preparation for confirmation impelled her finally away
from Lutheran Christianity. She has spoken of it not only
in the autobiographical fragment contained in the book
They Sought the Ancient Paths (De søkte de gamle stier, 1936),
but also in the description of Rose Wegener's confirmation
in *Spring* (1914). What first caused her revolt against
Lutheranism was its treatment of the seventh command-
ment. Even as a schoolgirl she had recoiled from what
Luther wrote about virginity, and she was now strengthened
in her opposition. She got the impression that, yes, chastity
was to be recommended, but at the same time it was unfor-
tunate, almost ridiculous, if a woman became an old maid.
Chastity came to be regarded as something negative, not
as a positive virtue, implying perhaps a development of
spiritual possibilities with a higher aim than simply that of
being a useful asset in the marriage market. In this contact
with the world of religion she received in effect no impression of the exalted and saintly. God was nearest to being
a comfortable family god from Homansbyen.

After Ingvald Undset's death, the financial circumstances
of the family were extremely trying. But rich as the traditions

within the home were, poverty could yet help to increase their perception of the non-material values of life.
She was embarrassed, she says in *Eleven Years,* when her
mother went into a shop and kept on asking how much
everything cost until she found something cheap enough to
buy,—or else went away without a purchase. But she was
ashamed of being ashamed! She understood quite clearly
"that the most joyless form of poverty is that where submission is made without protest to the opinion which considers it a shameful thing to be poor. She did not want to
submit to such an assessment of life's values, but at the
same time she felt that something inside her was yielding
under the pressure of circumstance. She knew that, in a
way, she too would have dearly liked to be invited to the
'fine rich houses', though she knew she would never enjoy
herself in them, the people were so boring. And she was
ashamed of herself because she had become the same as
they" (*Eleven Years*). But in reality she had not become and
was never to become the same.

When Sigrid Undset had taken her middle-school leaving
examination, Ragna Nielsen offered her the chance to stay
at school to study for matriculation. She thought however
that she could not accept this generous offer of a free place
with a clear conscience, now that she felt herself so remote
from the ideas in which Ragna Nielsen believed so ardently.
In any case she had no real desire to stay on at school:
as was said before, she wanted to be a painter. From
infancy she had received every impression so intensely, with
such definition and such delight, that the discipline of
fixing them in colour must have stirred the creative artistic
impulse within her.

Nevertheless, she still had to earn her living, and she went
to the Commercial College. At this time she came into contact with Dea Forsberg, a Swedish girl of the same age, through
a correspondence arranged by *Urd* and the Swedish young
people's paper, *Kamraten*. She introduced herself to her in

29

a letter which contained the following humorous self-portrait: "In character I am fanciful and vain, believing once that I had a good head and considered talented at school, but now proving I am nothing of the kind at the Commercial College I attend. At first it was intended that I should become a student, but I had no wish for that, and consequently I was put here, where they are busy in accomplishing my speedy decease."

Her certificate from the Commercial College was not superlatively good, but with the help of some good friends she found an office post with Chr. Wisbech, an agent for A.E.G. Sigrid Undset worked in an office for ten years and three months, an important part of her life and essential in her development as a writer. Office-work was not exactly to her taste. She liked none of the work she had to do, she used to say, except housework; and she often said how terrible she thought it was to be confined behind a desk. To have to be on the spot, for example, as soon as she was rung for! But she proved an excellent secretary, almost indispensable, not least because of her phenomenal powers of memory. She carried everything in her head down to the last detail. She never lost her imperturbable tranquillity. One of her colleagues relates that, if an attack of nerves had disorganised the rest of the office, Sigrid Undset would still remain at her work, calm and immovable. One mid-morning break she sat and chuckled over something she was reading. It was a piece she had written herself, a description of actual events, amongst them the arrival of the King in 1905. She read it to the others. It was written with such "warmth and humour", say her colleagues, "that we could not help interrupting: 'Good Heavens! Why don't you write instead of sitting in an office?'"

She had begun to feel seriously that she wanted to write. It was clear to her that her real powers as an artist lay in that medium. In many ways a completely novel world